A FINE MESS!

Verbal and Visual Gems from
THE CRAZY WORLD OF LAUREL & HARDY

A Hal Roach—Jay Ward Production

Edited by
Richard J. Anobile

A DARIEN HOUSE BOOK

DISTRIBUTED BY CROWN PUBLISHERS, INC.
NEW YORK, NEW YORK

A DARIEN HOUSE BOOK

Cover art by Al Hirschfeld.
Mr. Hirschfeld is represented exclusively by
the Margo Feiden Galleries, New York City.

Design by Harry Chester Associates

DISTRIBUTED BY:
CROWN PUBLISHERS, INC.
419 PARK AVENUE SOUTH
NEW YORK, NEW YORK 10016

ISBN 0-517-524-384

Library of Congress Catalogue Card Number: 75-18996

Printed in the United States of America

THE CRAZY WORLD OF LAUREL & HARDY

A Hal Roach-Jay Ward Production

EXECUTIVE PRODUCERS:	Jay Ward, Bill Scott
PRODUCER:	Hal Roach
ASSOCIATE PRODUCER:	Raymond Rohauer
SCENARIO:	Bill Scott
FILM EDITORS:	Skip Craig, Roger Donley
MUSIC:	Jerry Fielding
NARRATED BY:	Garry Moore
LENGTH:	83 minutes

This feature motion picture can be viewed and enjoyed in its entirety at your local theatre or on your television screen. For information regarding theatrical, non-theatrical and television rights throughout the world, contact: Jay Ward Productions, Inc., 8218 Sunset Boulevard, Los Angeles, California 90046, or its representative Mr. Raymond Rohauer, 44 West 62nd Street, Suite 16B, New York City 10023 (Telephone 212-765-8262).

Jay Ward Productions Inc. acknowledges the kind cooperation of Mr. Hal Roach, Sr., Mr. Herbert R. Gelbspan, Hal Roach Studios, Inc. and the trustees for Hal Roach Studios for helping to bring the CRAZY WORLD OF LAUREL & HARDY to life.

THE CRAZY WORLD OF LAUREL & HARDY was produced by Hal Roach in 1965 in association with Jay Ward Productions Inc. The resulting film was shown at the Berlin Film Festival in 1965. Hal Roach was honored for his fifty years in films at the Berlin Film Festival by being presented the coveted medallion C.I.D.A.L.C. Award (*Committee of International Diffusion for the Arts and Letters*) by its President Mr. N. Pillat.

THE CRAZY WORLD OF LAUREL & HARDY, under the expert tutelage of Hal Roach himself, was judiciously viewed and edited from more than 50 Laurel and Hardy films of the sound and silent era in order to create this hilarious distillation of the very essence of their humor. In doing so this film has taken a new and promising approach. Instead of merely stringing together a number of funny scenes from funny pictures, this film in many cases reduces entire pictures to short sequences while keeping intact their stories and their extravagant tomfoolery. The film also examines some of the artful devices which helped to create the "world" of these two giants of comedy—their preposterous preoccupation with small, everyday items like hats and doors; and their breezy, offhand, and cavalier treatment of large and aggressive things like automobiles and machinery.

Introduction

The first book in this comedy classics series was *Why a Duck?* Published in 1970, it turned out to be an extraordinary success. No doubt that success was due to the increasing popularity of the Marx Bros. Since the publication of *Why A Duck?* I have refined the frame blowup technique and have added books on Fields, Abbott and Costello and more Marx Bros. to this series.

I am pleased with the popularity of the series and flattered by the many readers who have taken the time and trouble to write to me. I am not always able to answer each letter but contact with the followers of this series has made me keenly aware of their feelings. A FINE MESS is my answer to the hundreds of letters I have received requesting a frame blowup treatment of Stan Laurel and Oliver Hardy.

We finally have it due to the fact that Jay Ward Productions produced a compilation film titled *The Crazy World of Laurel & Hardy.* The scenes in this book and its sequel are culled from that compilation film.

My first encounter with Laurel and Hardy came when I was no more than seven years old. Television was still a novelty and I spent hours soaking up just about everything imaginable. One of my favorite shows was "Joe Franklin's Memory Lane." It usually aired in the early morning over WOR-TV. It was a local show seen only in the New York area. Franklin is a nostalgia freak and his program was a potpourri of old recordings, guests and, my favorite, film clips. Usually the clips were those of some obscure silent film comedian but on numerous occasions viewers would be treated to the likes of Buster Keaton, Charlie Chaplin, Harold Lloyd and Laurel and Hardy.

Looking back over these years I now realize that it was the film clips Franklin presented which were directly responsible for my interest in film comedy. This eventually spawned my further interest in all film. The Franklin show continued (and still does today) and my next dose of Laurel and Hardy came while I was assistant to Raymond Rohauer who was then the film curator at the Gallery of Modern Art in New York City. During the presentation of a Laurel and Hardy series, I was able to see virtually their entire film output and, in addition, meet the man who not only brought them together, but who also produced most of their classic films, Hal Roach, Sr.

I consider Laurel and Hardy superior film comedians second to none. Chaplin is good, but overrated. In fact, I always place Chaplin third behind Buster Keaton in any discussion I have about early film comedy. But that is another matter which I will take up in future books. Compiling this book has simply reinforced my feelings about fat and skinny. Their humor is timeless; its execution superb. The grace with which they involve themselves in and extricate themselves from chaotic situations can only be compared with the finest work of Nureyev and Fontaine.

As I slowed down my moviola and carefully watched each frame slip by, I could sense the precise preparation which had to go into the making of each and every Laurel and Hardy film. Every move is flawlessly orchestrated. Each turn and twist is logical though the audience is always assured that every manipulation will only drive the pair further into their predicament. And here is the key. No audience, no matter how young, can help but feel superior to Stan and Ollie.

The audience sits helplessly, usually bowled over with laughter, as the pair compound previous errors. They are lovable. You want to help them but you can't. You must just sit in your seat as those two average guys on screen find their own way through the messes they themselves create.

Every disaster is anticipated by the audience. It's that anticipation which heightens our laughter. We know everything which will happen moments before it ever does. Yet, as in a dream we cannot control, we simply resign ourselves to the fact that what we are seeing on screen might be a slight glimpse into an understanding of our own selves.

Laurel and Hardy are all of us, more so than the little tramp. We are not angry and neither are Mr. Laurel and Mr. Hardy. Like us, they are simply struggling to wean the best out of a life which they inadvertently chose but which they cannot understand. We have all fallen prey to get-rich-quick schemes, easy ways out and shortcuts. Somewhere in the back of our minds we all know they never work, yet the lure of a pot of gold at the end of the rainbow is always too strong to ignore. We have tried to charm another person; to give the image we feel will most appeal to that person. Yet we know that, in the end, we shall have to be ourselves. This is Laurel and Hardy. These are their themes, over and over and over again.

Their humor is that of mankind and was valid when they first performed it, is valid today and will be valid for your children and theirs. But by that time I assume each and every home will have cassette film libraries which will put Laurel and Hardy and all film classics in daily reach of everyone.

Though I could not personally cull through each and every film of Laurel and Hardy as I have been able to do with other subjects, I am satisfied that the sequences I have selected from *The Crazy World of Laurel and Hardy* are the cream of the cream. There is very little dialogue in a Laurel and Hardy movie. The term "talkie" just doesn't apply to them. Everything we understand from their humor is gotten visually. And everything they do is dependent upon flawless timing and a rapport with their audience. It is no accident that Stan and Ollie both take every opportunity to look out at their audience. A cardinal rule of filmmaking is thus consistently broken. But they are *the* exception.

Keeping this in mind I have allowed myself a luxury with Laurel and Hardy that I have worked to shed as I grew more skillful in compiling these books. Usually, I try to be as economical as possible with my frame selection. Only Fields has been an exception. And even there I did not go far astray. Only enough to convey Fields' lackadaisical attitude about his life.

But here I have thrown caution to the winds and have allowed myself as many blowups of frames necessary to convey Laurel and Hardy's sense of rhythm. I noticed that every seemingly insignificant piece of action was important to laying the foundation for the always inevitable disaster. Thus, I have taken pains to capture every look, every glance and every bit of body action necessary to the understanding of where the pair is headed in a given scene.

Here then are over 1000 frame blowups from sequences from the films of Laurel and Hardy. It is an accurate record of each scene. The photos are not a bunch of tired publicity shots, but rather blowups taken directly from the actual film. All the dialogue is placed exactly where it was spoken. It is my hope that this volume will form a lasting record of the art of Laurel and Hardy.

Richard J. Anobile
Los Angeles
June 1975

NOTE TO THE READER

You will notice a fuzziness or graininess in some photos. This is due to the fact that *every* photo is a blowup of the individual frames of the film itself. All possible means have been taken to insure clarity but inconsistencies in negative quality of this compilation of 40-year-old films account for the variations of photo densities you will observe. These frames, in addition to their age and fragile state, were, of course, meant to be seen at rapid speed on a screen; by arresting the action at a single frame, we have, necessarily and artificially, frozen that scene to better view it in book form. But at the same time we have also exposed all the dirt, grains and imperfections which the theatre viewer would not normally see. However, only in this manner, by going directly to the film rather than using publicity shots or stills, could the authenticity of the routines be preserved.

Also, in keeping as true to the film as possible, lap dissolves and fades were left in where necessary. The effect of a lap dissolve to the reader will be the appearance of two seemingly superimposed photos. The purpose here, as it was the director's, is to bridge the time and place gap between two scenes.

ACKNOWLEDGMENTS

I would like to take this opportunity to thank those individuals and corporations who helped to make this book possible.

The rights to produce this book were granted to us by Jay Ward Productions, Inc. I would especially like to acknowledge the assistance of Mr. Jay Ward in seeing that the necessary materials were made available for my use. I would also like to thank the Associate Producer of *The Crazy World of Laurel & Hardy* Mr. Raymond Rohauer, for his invaluable aid in this project.

Alyne Model, George Norris and Jan Kohn of Riverside Film Associates accurately transferred my marks to the negative materials. All blowups were produced by Vita Print Corp. in New York under the watchful eye of Saul Jaffee. Harry Chester was once again responsible for the design. And Helen Garfinkle worked hard to see that my wires didn't get crossed.

Above all, one must acknowledge the unique contribution of the individual who had the foresight to bring this comedy team together; who produced all the films upon which this compilation is based; who therefore made this book possible—the incomparable Hal Roach, Sr.

—Richard J. Anobile

GOING BYE-BYE «1934»

Mr. Hardy introduces Mr. Laurel.

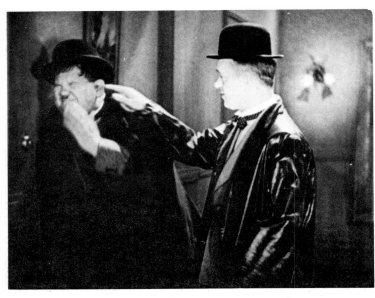 

14

Hardy: How do you do? We're the gentlemen you're going East with.

Woman: Oh, won't you come in?

Hardy: Eh, flowers for you.

ardy: I'm Mr. Hardy.

Hardy: And . . .

ardy: I'm Mr. Hardy.

Hardy: As I was saying,

Hardy: I'm Mr. Hardy.

Hardy: This is my friend, Mr. Laurel.

SWISS MISS

◄ 1938 ►

Chicken plucking
ain't half-bad
if one can
get into
the proper
spirits.

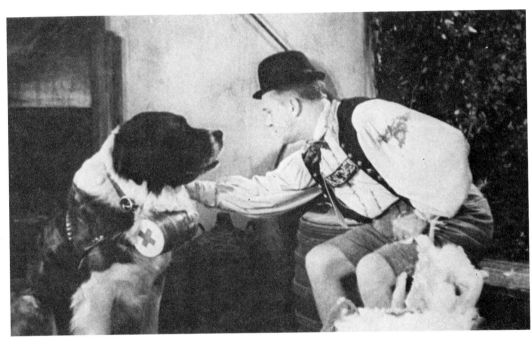

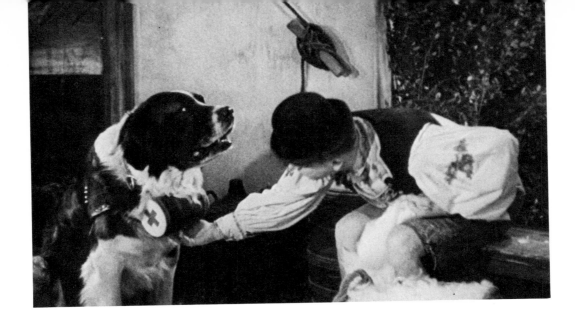

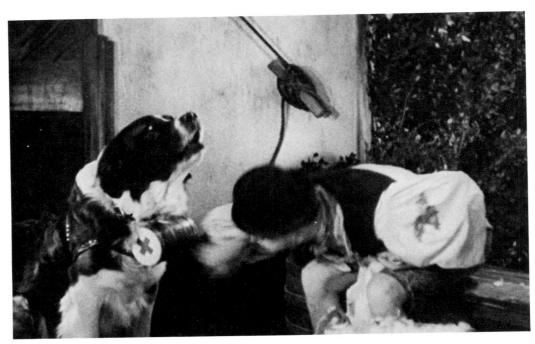

43

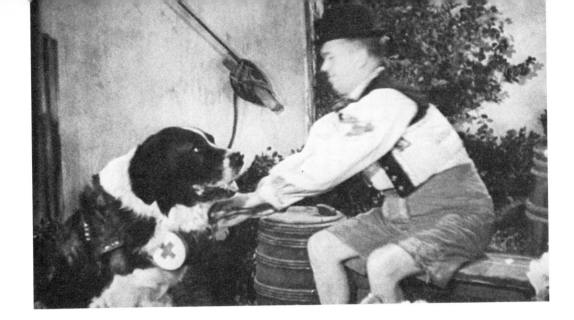

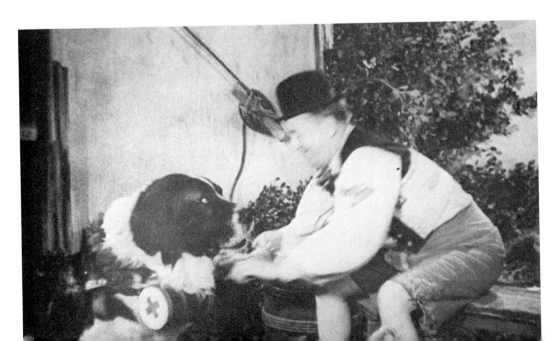

Laurel:
Oh, oh!

Laurel: Help!

Laurel: I'm exhausted.

Laurel: Oh, help!

Laurel: Help!

Laurel: Oh, help.

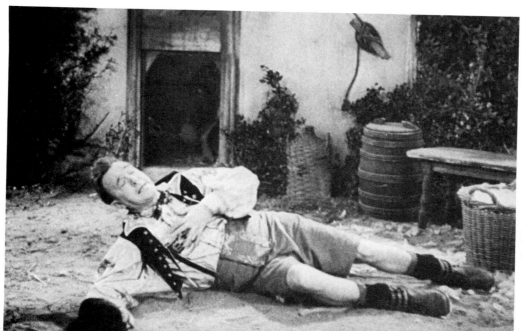

Laurel: I'm exhausted!

Laurel: Help!

Laurel: Help. I'm freezing to death!

71

Laurel:
Help, help!

Laurel:
Help.

Laurel:
Help.

Laurel:
Help.

Laurel:
Help!

Laurel:
Ah!

Laurel:
Help!

GOING BYE-BYE

« 1934 »

A short take . . .

Laurel: What are you doing in there?

THE MUSIC BOX ·1932·

For their performance and endurance in this short film,
Laurel & Hardy received their one and only Academy Award.
Following are excerpts highlighting their frustrating battle
with a stubborn player piano.

Hardy: Whoa!

Hardy: Pardon me, Mr. Postman.

Postman: Yes, sir.

Hardy: Can you tell me where 1127 Walnut Avenue is?

Postman: 1127 Walnut Avenue?
Hardy: Yes, sir.

Postman: That's the house up there.

Postman: Right on top of the stoop.

Hardy: Steady Susie.

Hardy: Heave!

Laurel: Ho!

ardy: Heave!

Laurel: Ho!

Hardy: Heave!

Laurel: Ho!

Nurse:
Could you
gentlemen
please let
me pass?

Hardy:
Why certainly,
ma'am.

Hardy:
Come on.

Hardy: Just
a moment.
Maybe I can
help.

89

94

Nurse:
Ha ha
ha ha ha!

Nurse: Ha ha ha ha ha!

Nurse:
Ha ha ha
ha ha!

Nurse: Of all the dumb.

Nurse: Things!

Nurse: Ha, ha, ha.

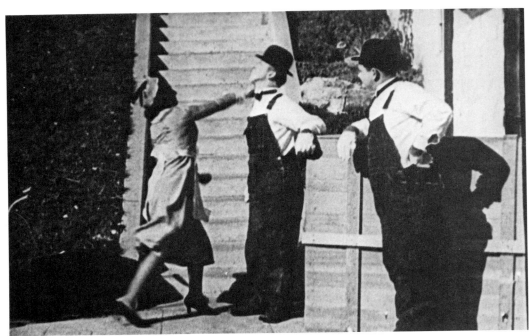

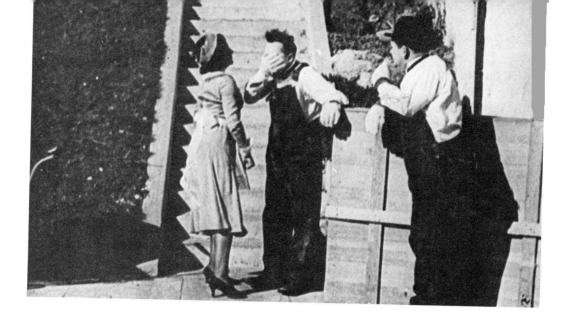

Hardy:
Ha ha ha ha.

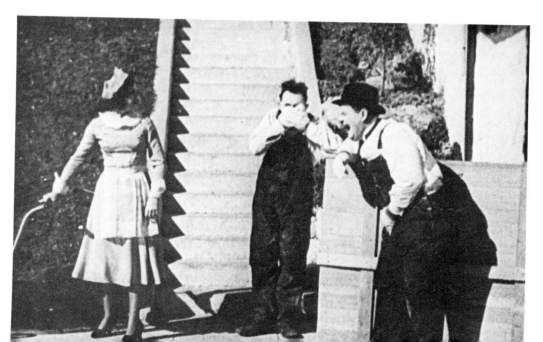

Hardy: Heave!

Laurel: Ho!

Hardy: Heave!
Laurel: Ho!

111

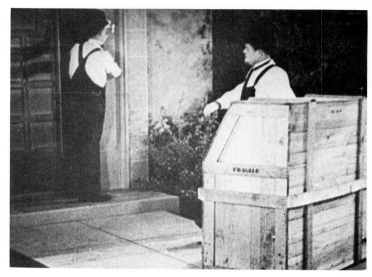

   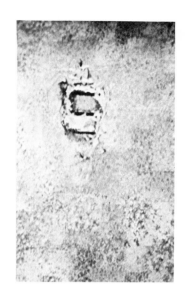

Laurel: Well, I guess we have to take it back.

rdy: Why!

Laurel: There's nobody home.

Hardy: Where there's a will, there's a way.

Hardy: We'll take the piano.

Hardy: Through the window.

Hardy: Down the stairs and place it in the living room.

Hardy: You find a ladder and I'll get the block and tackle.

Hardy: Hm-hm-hmm!

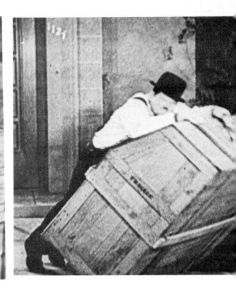

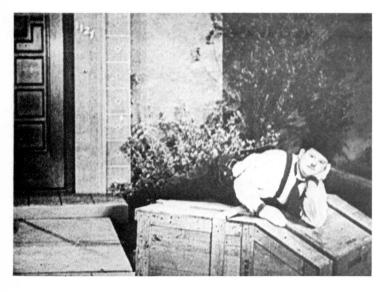

Hardy: Oh!

Hardy: Why don't you watch what you're doing.

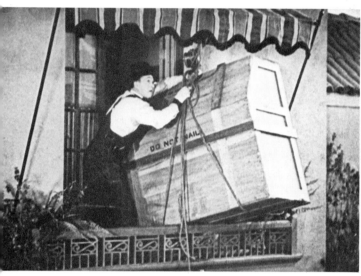

Hardy: Ohh!

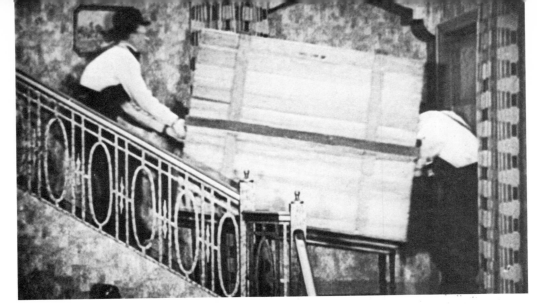

Hardy: Ohh!

Hardy: Get that piano out of there while I find a place to put it.

Hardy: I'll get it out!

TOWED IN A HOLE ‹1932›

"Always tamper with success" is a recurrent Laurel & Hardy motto.

LAUREL AND HARDY
FRESH FISH
CRABS A SPECIALITY

Hardy: Fresh fish!

Hardy:
Hah-ha!

Hardy:
Boy oh boy!

Hardy: For the first time in our lives we're a success.

Laurel: You know, Ollie, I've been thinking.

Hardy: What about?

Laurel: I know how we could make a lot more money.

Hardy: How?

Laurel: Well, if we caught our own fish we wouldn't have to pay for it.

Laurel: Then whoever we sold it to . . .

Laurel: . . . it would be clear profit.

Hardy: Tell me that again.

Laurel: Well. If you caught a fish, whoever you sold it to they wouldn't have to pay for it.

Laurel: Then the profits . . .

Laurel: they go to the fish if a . . .

Hardy: I know exactly what you mean.

ardy: Your idea is to eliminate the middleman.

Laurel: Hey, Ollie!

Hardy: What?

Laurel: The boat's full of water.

Hardy: Alright. You go ahead and scrub the deck. I'll look for the leaks when I've finished this painting.

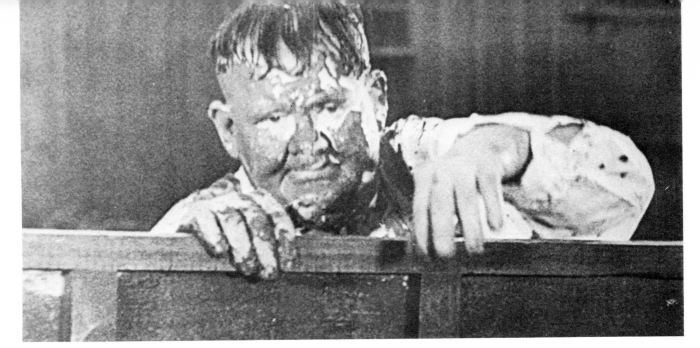

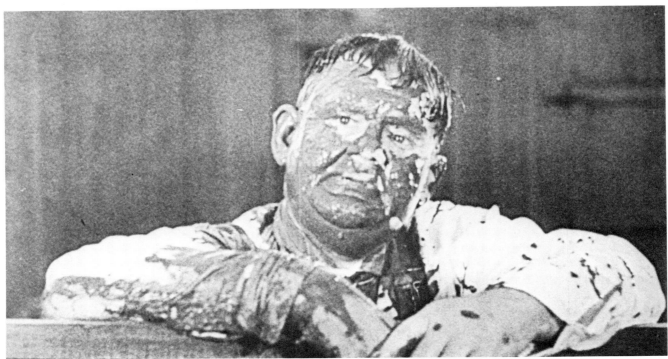

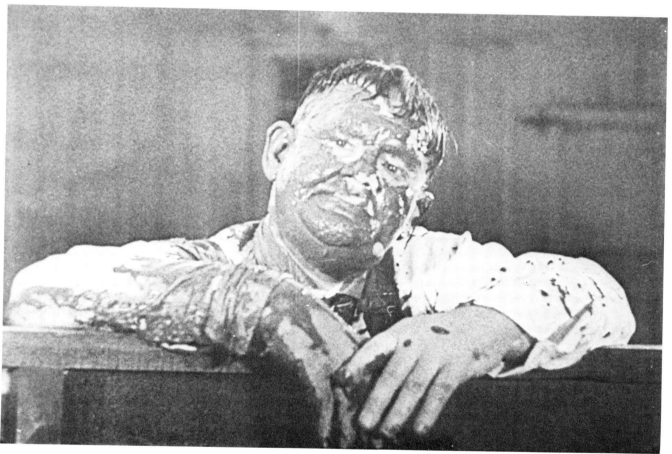

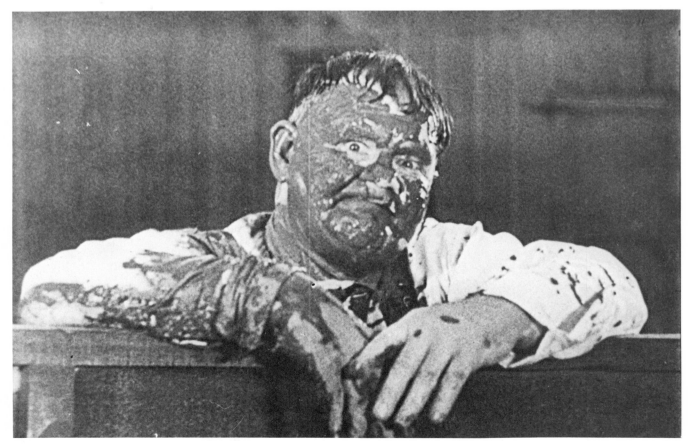

 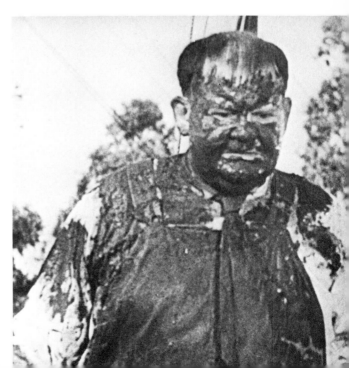

Laurel: What'd you put that stuff on your face for?

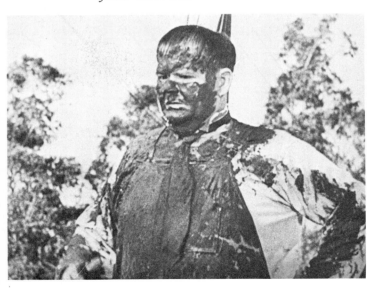

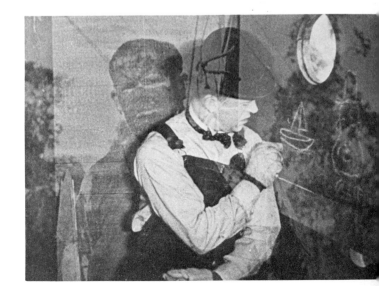

Laurel: Ollie!

Hardy: I told you that I didn't want to talk to you!

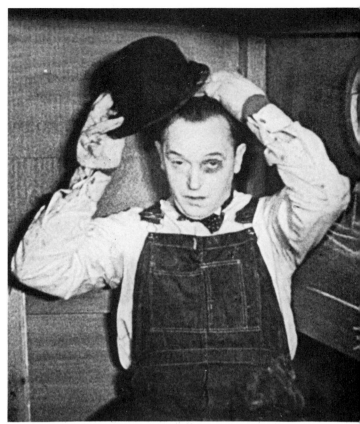

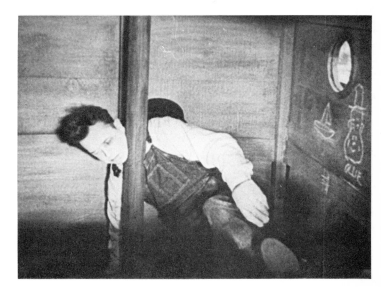

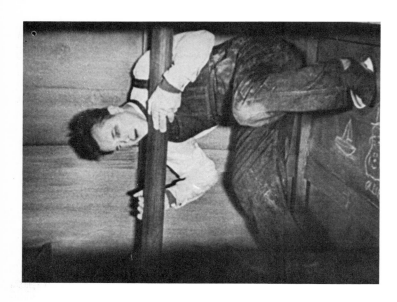

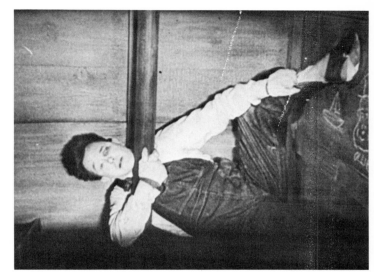

187

Laurel: Why don't you put the sail up?

194

BUSY BODIES
◄ 1933 ►

In the real world,
a saw mill is the last place
for Laurel and Hardy
to be near. Yet in this
sequence, they *work* there.

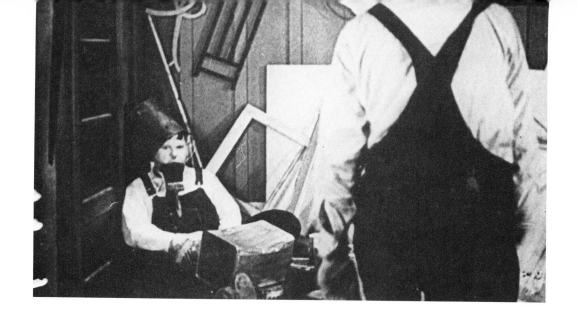

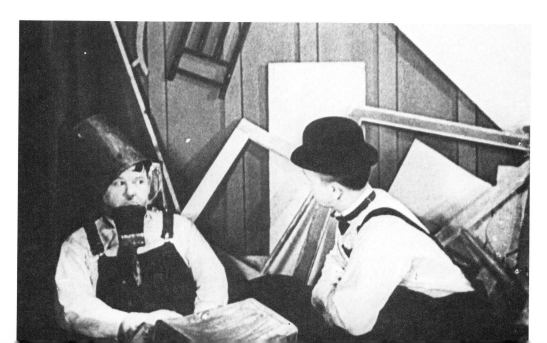

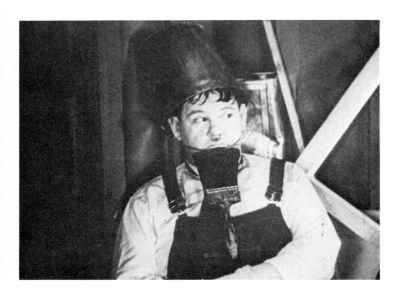

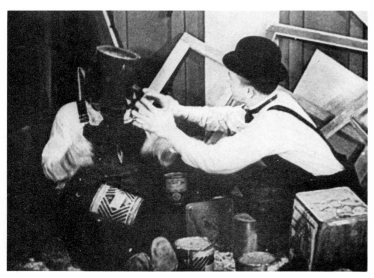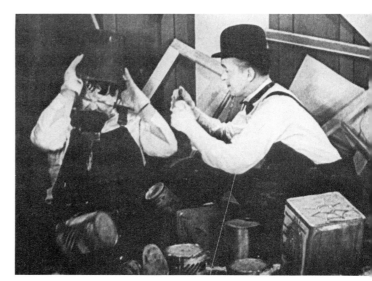

Man: Hey, will you hang this coat in the closet for me?

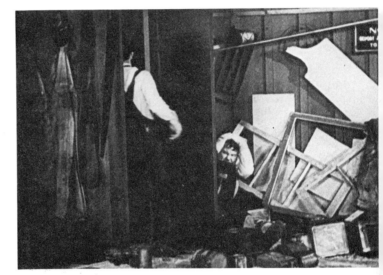

Hardy: Ow!

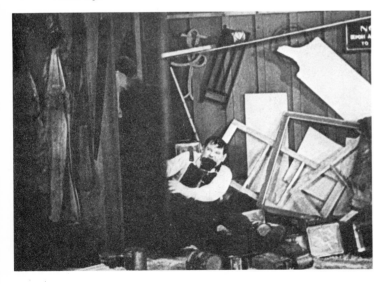

Hardy: Ow!

Hardy: Ohh!

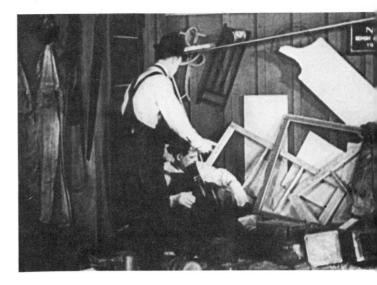 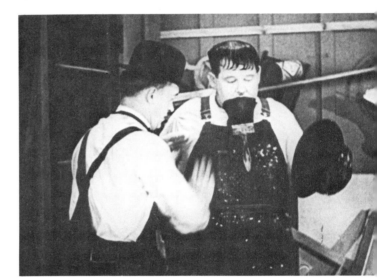

 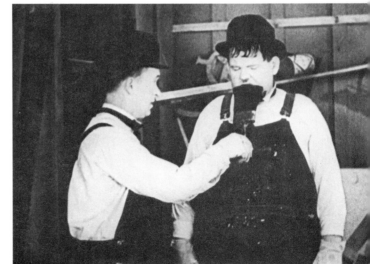

 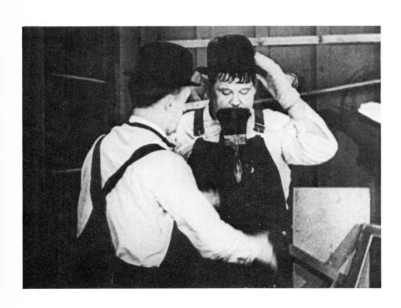

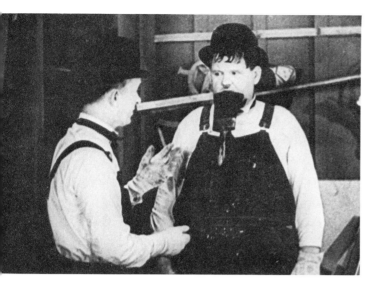

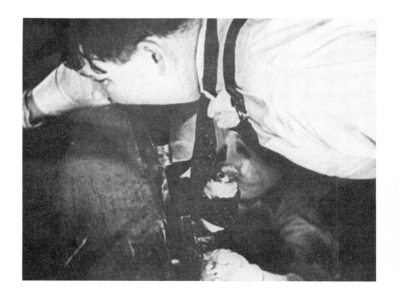

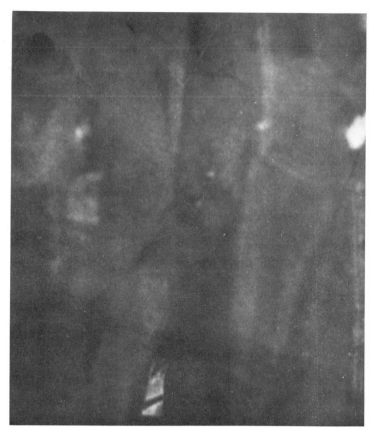

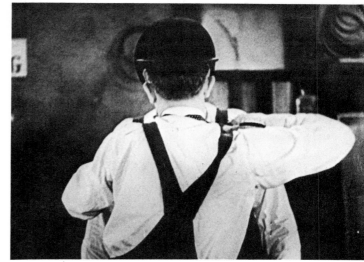

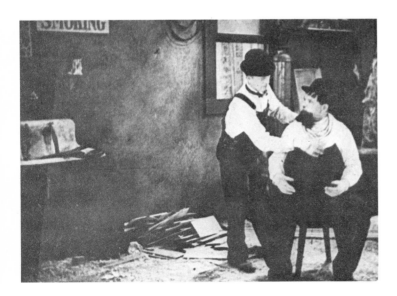

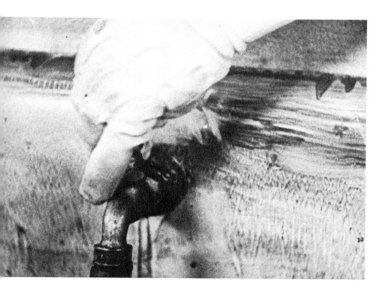

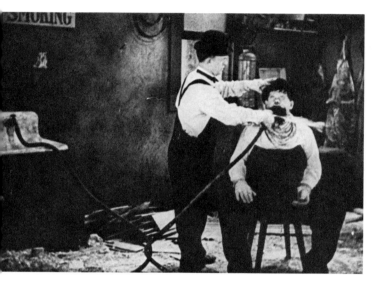

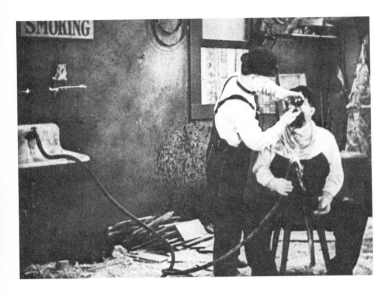

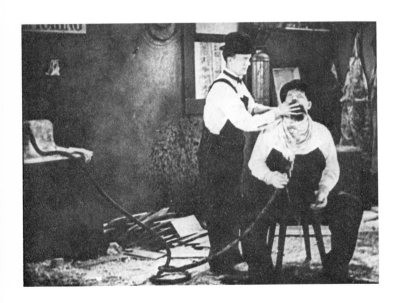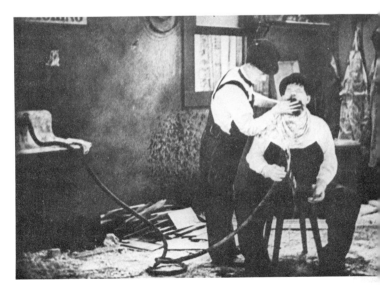

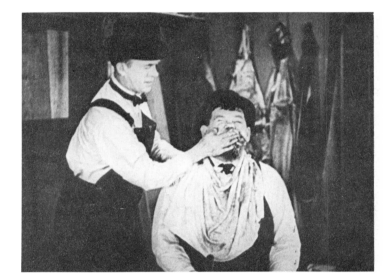

Hardy: Thank you.

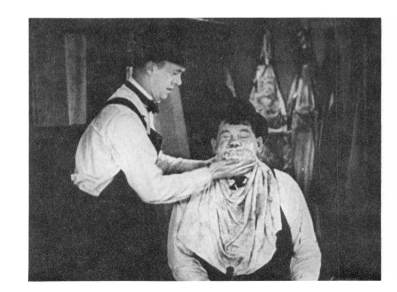

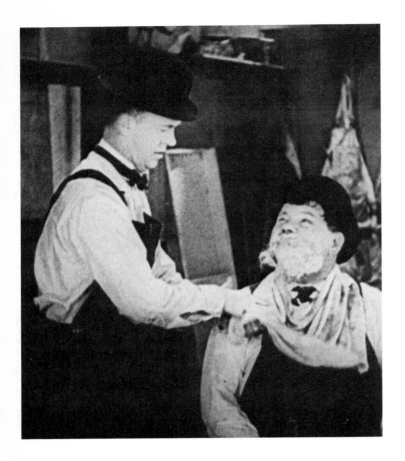

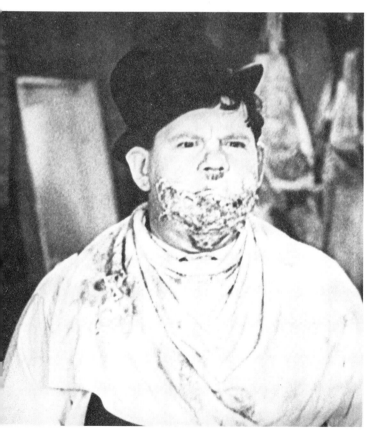

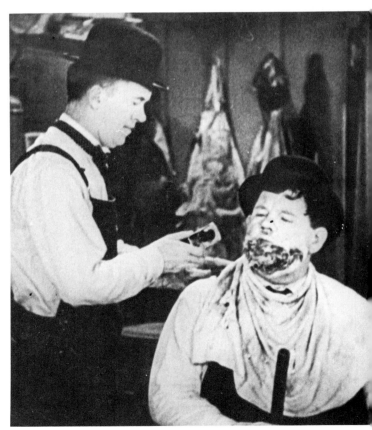

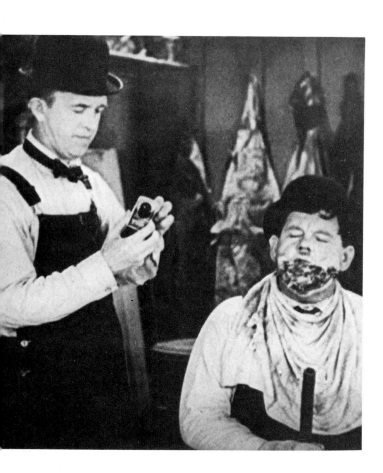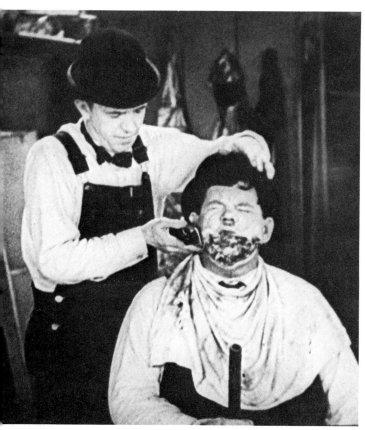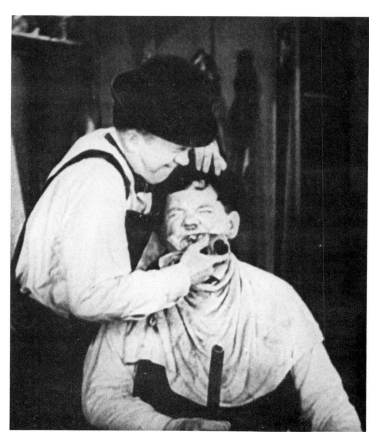

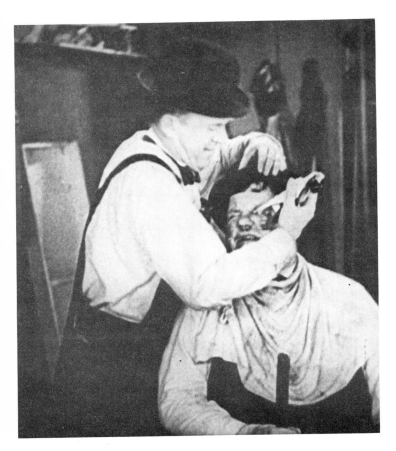

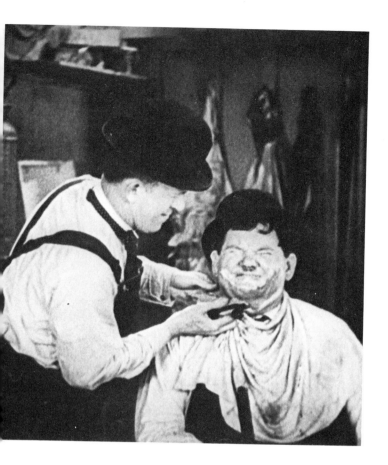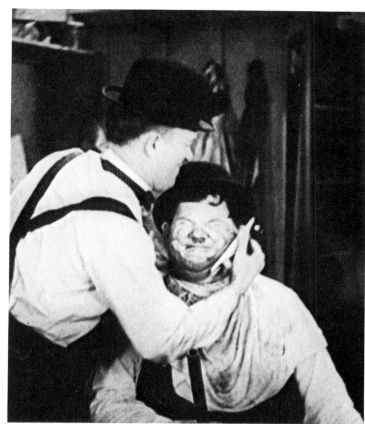

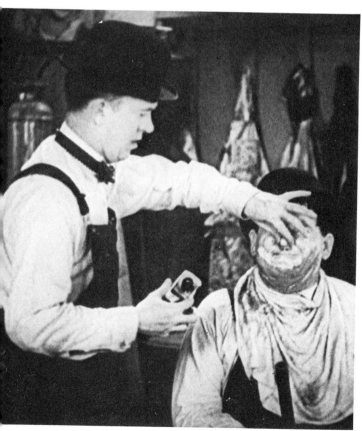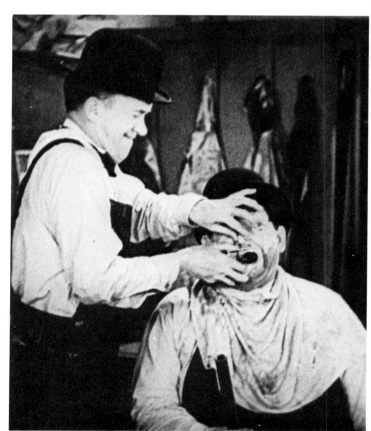

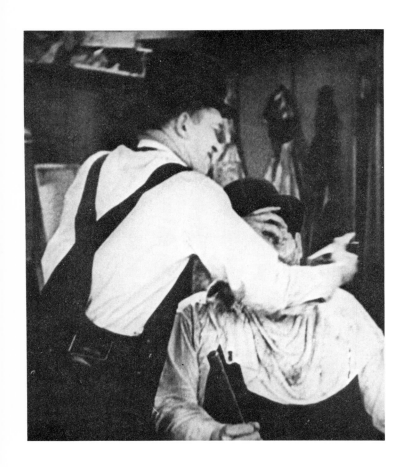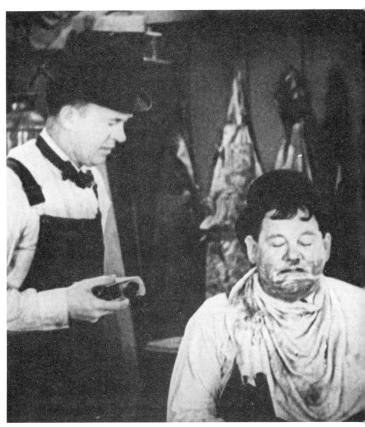

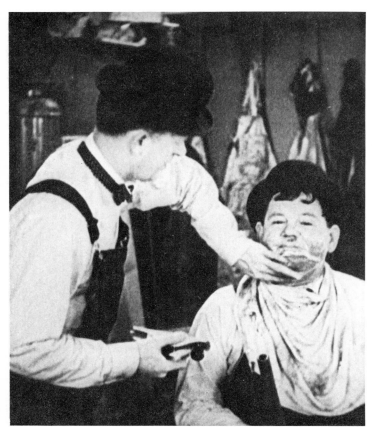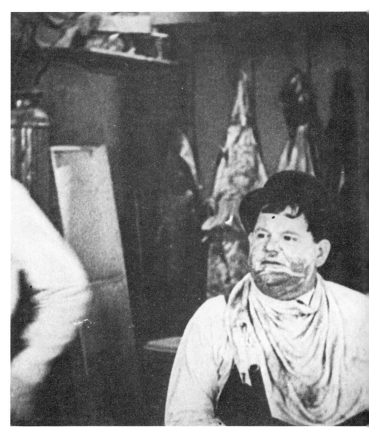

Hardy: Ohh!

Hardy: Ah, ah, ah.

Hardy: Oh, oh, oh.

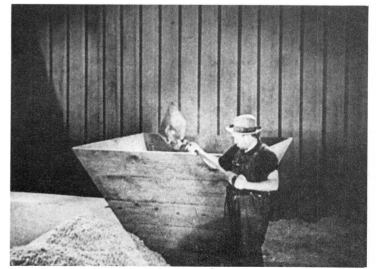

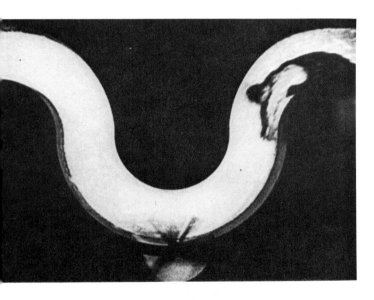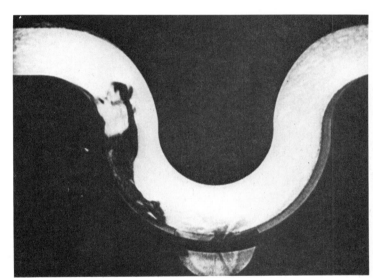

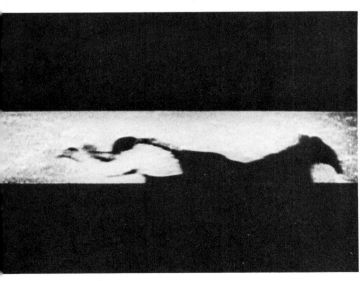

 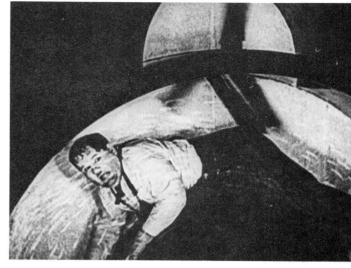

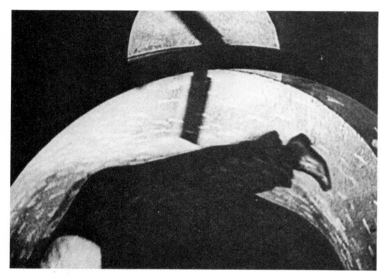 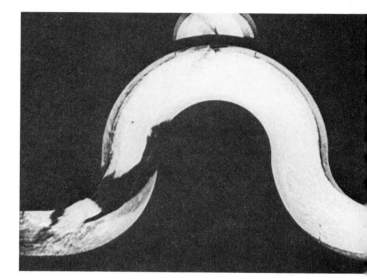

Laurel: You dropped your hat!

Hardy: Thank you.

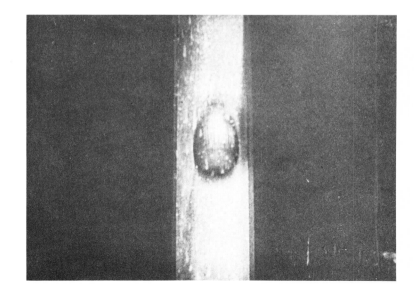

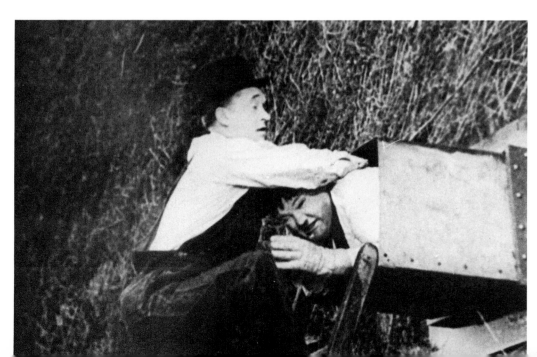

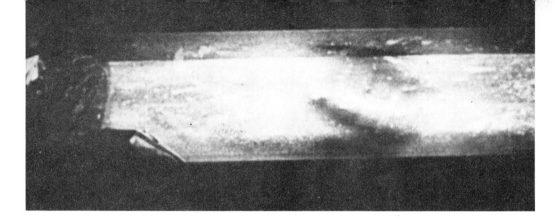

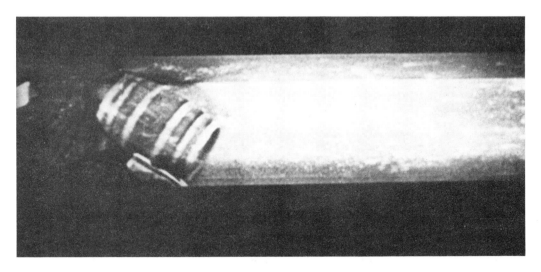

248

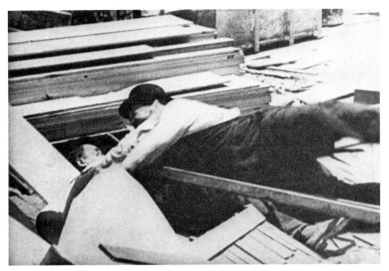

Hardy: Will you let go of my ears.

Laurel: Come in!